# THE LORD AND THE
# GENERAL DIN OF THE WORLD

■

# THE
# LORD
## AND THE
# GENERAL
# DIN
## OF THE
# WORLD

## POEMS
# Jane Mead

*Winner of the 1995*
*Kathryn A. Morton Prize in Poetry*
*Selected by Philip Levine*

SARABANDE BOOKS
LOUISVILLE, KENTUCKY

Managing Editor
Sarabande Books, Inc.
2234 Dundee Road, Suite 200
Louisville, KY 40205

Elvis Costello's lyrics in stanza five and seven of "In the Parking Lot at the
Junior College on the Eve of a Presidential Election" are reprinted courtesy of
Plangent Visions Music Limited.

Hoover Factory (Costello)
© 1980 Plangent Visions Music Limited

Cover Photograph: *The Great Columns, Cathedral of Saint John the Divine*
by Hal Conroy
C. Harrison Co., Inc.
1300 South Graham Street
Charlotte, North Carolina 28203

Cover and Interior Design by Charles Casey Martin

Manufactured in the United States of America
This book is printed on acid-free paper.

Sarabande Books is a non-profit literary organization.

Library of Congress Cataloging-in-Publication Data
Mead, Jane, 1958–
    The Lord and the general din of the world / Jane Mead.
        p.    cm.
    ISBN 0-9641151-0-7 (cloth). — ISBN 0-9641151-1-5 (pbk.)
    I. Title.
    PS3563.E165L67    1996
    811'.54—dc20                                          95-23868
                                                            CIP

*For Nancy Morgan Whitaker*
*and*
*For Giles Willis Mead*

*With Love*

# Table of Contents

## THREE

# Foreword

In an early review of William Carlos Williams' great book, Randall Jarrell wrote, "The subject of *Paterson* is: How can you tell the truth about things?—that is, how can you find a language so close to the world that the world can be represented and understood in it?" That search for language is the same one Jane Mead conducts in her extraordinary first book *The Lord and the General Din of the World*, but the truths Mead tells have less to do with the sights, smells, and sounds of a place and far more to do with the taste of loss, grief, and madness in a community that has spun out of control. In many of her poems that community is a community of two rather than a city, and we, the readers, eavesdrop on a passionate internalized debate that is about no more and no less than the question of whether or not we should live and, should we choose to, how we might go about it.

There are no easy answers in the world in which Mead has grown into her difficult adulthood, but in her poems the natural world is bodied forth in its splendor and beauty and we live just on the brink of joining it. It is a frontier she rarely crosses:

> I'm the one who's always fasting
> as if God would then come in,
> the one with twigs snarled in her hair
> watching a penful of pigs.
> They lie in the mud shitting themselves
> and squinting at me. I love them
> because nothing can do *pig* as well as pig
> and I am lost and do not know who I am, or if
> life has anything to do with prayer.
>                    ("Between Self and Century")

But even on her side of the frontier between the sacred natural world and the clouded human one certain truths must be stated, and she states them with clarity and assurance in one of the most startling poems in the collection, "Concerning That Prayer I Cannot Make":

Listen—
all you bare trees
burrs
brambles
pile of twigs
red and green lights flashing
muddy bottle shards
shoe half buried—listen

listen, I am holy.

These poems are driven forward by the knowledge that we could hear the meaning of the world in all things, including ourselves, if only we were given the power to listen. "Lord," she asks in the title poem, "is the general din of the world your own?" This "steady grating," as she calls it, is made up of the united voices of all that otherwise might be inconsequential—a plastic bottle, a concrete gutter, tiny waves in a swimming pool—as well as the agonized cries of a human voice.

Even in their most placid moments these poems teeter on the edge of violence as the poet's mind circles around a center of dread. At a poetry lounge (whatever that is) in Berkeley, Mead observes a man reading English pastoral poetry to himself and wonders if the smooth iambs soothe him. Though Mead is immersed in poetry, it is her allergies she is aware of. She wonders if the birds have appeared yet in those pastoral poems, but because her mind is always centered on catastrophe the mere suggestion of larks and nightingales reminds her of Flanders and Picardy, the sites of the horrendous battles of WW I. "The Man in the Poetry Lounge" is a poem that questions the value of poetry itself; it contains no final answer.

Contemplating the late poetry of Thomas Hardy, the English poet Edward Thomas wrote that Hardy's work contained "ninety-nine reasons for not living. Yet it is not a book of despair." I doubt there are ninety-nine reasons in this collection, though it is not a joyous book—very few contemporary poetry collections are—but it too is not a cause for despair. It is because in these poems we suffer a world of madness, addiction, and death that the moments of redemption are so charged and significant. In "After Detox" she writes:

> In the morning, sitting in my nightgown by the window,
> I watch the light seep around the corners of Glen's Garage.
> Yellow, orange, blue. Colors of the rainbow
> or the sky rising. Colors on the rusted plates
> on the rusted cars. Cars with their toes turned up,
> tires sold, fenders missing. Cars from all over, with maps
> of stars on the windshields where heads have smashed.

As you can hear, Mead is determined not to let us off easily; even the most serene moments are stained with the human, but these poems possess the uncanny ability to discover beauty where we almost never see it, in the least honored and most despised places.

Finally, it should be stated emphatically: This is poetry. Perhaps it does not contain a surplus of those details we associate with poetry. There are no swains here, though there is a man at the LaGuardia Airport holding an iris. You won't find elms, but there are cottonwoods. The sea makes an appearance. Children enter, a blood-stained needle, vineyards, dying young men, a truckload of chickens on the way to market, a father armed and threatening. Mead's work does not rely on a special or exalted vocabulary. You won't find those "auras" or "angels" that turn up so often in today's fashionable poetry. There is not a single Buddha in the entire collection, but the language is as alive and unpredictable as a cat, though sometimes in its stubbornness and truculence it reminds one more of a badger:

> If I put in the part about my mother
> and step-father fighting, if I describe
> —perfectly—his body in action,
> his shadow on the wall behind him,
> or add the bit about it all boiling down
> to inquisitions in the rational morning—as in
> whose dark anus holds the safe-box key—
> will we have a story with a meaning?
>                          ("LaGuardia, the Story")

Her language is a constant source of delight and alarm. It seldom crosses the page in order to entertain us. It prefers to leap out of its own darkness with the suddenness of something wild and catch us by the throat. It is what poetry has always been, risky and untamable.

*Philip Levine*
*Fresno, July 1995*

# THE LORD AND THE
# GENERAL DIN OF THE WORLD

■

# Concerning That Prayer I Cannot Make

Jesus, I am cruelly lonely
and I do not know what I have done
nor do I suspect that you will answer me.

And, what is more, I have spent
these bare months bargaining
with my soul as if I could make her
promise to love me when now it seems
that what I meant when I said "soul"
was that the river reflects
the railway bridge just as the sky
says it should—it speaks *that* language.

I do not know who you are.

I come here every day
to be beneath this bridge,
to sit beside this river,
so I *must* have seen the way
the clouds just slide
under the rusty arch—
without snagging on the bolts,
how they are borne along on the dark water—
I must have noticed their fluent speed
and also how that tattered blue T-shirt
remains snagged on the crown
of the mostly sunk dead tree
despite the current's constant pulling.
Yes, somewhere in my mind there must
be the image of a sky blue T-shirt, caught,
and the white islands of ice flying by
and the light clouds flying slowly

under the bridge, though today the river's
fully melted.  I must have seen.

But I did not see.

I am not equal to my longing.
Somewhere there should be a place
the exact shape of my emptiness—
there should be a place
responsible for taking one back.
The river, of course, has no mercy—
it just lifts the dead fish
toward the sea.

Of course, of course.

What I *meant* when I said "soul"
was that there should be a place.

On the far bank the warehouse lights
blink red, then green, and all the yellow
machines with their rusted scoops and lifts
sit under a thin layer of sunny frost.

And look—
my own palm—
there, slowly rocking.
It is *my* pale palm—
palm where a black pebble
is turning and turning.

     Listen—
     all you bare trees

burrs
brambles
pile of twigs
red and green lights flashing
muddy bottle shards
shoe half buried—listen

listen, I am holy.

# • ONE •

# The Lord and the General Din of the World

The kids are shrieking at the edge of the pool,
their angelic faces twisting. They like
to shriek—they like to make the Great Dane bellow.
When he cannot stand it any longer, he jumps
the wall and chases them, still screaming, in.

And under all this now a steady grating—
a plastic bottle of blue cheese dressing
scraping up against the concrete gutter,
bobbing off the aqua, sun-flicked waves
the kids have made by jumping.

And there's a man here from Afghanistan
who hasn't cut his greasy hair since he was driven mad.
His name is Simon. He looks just like The Christ.
Walks up and down beside the pool, oblivious
to screams and barking. He gestures as he talks,
whispers and pontificates. No one is listening.

*Lord, is the general din of the world your own?*
*Something that is good in me is crumbling.*

Early this morning I walked out into the vineyard
where the sun hits the sunburnt grapeleaves
and the dusty grapes about to be harvested.
I felt something light then—the skittish joy
that is also a falling off from the world
to that place you can get to by fasting.

Simon marches by, then stops—and looks
at a stretch of bright green grass:
        "Is that shit?
        I thought so.

I have been here before.
They always hide the horses though."

*What holds me here destroys me as I go.*

# Fall

*for Aspen and Shaheen*

This morning I found
a used needle in the empty box
marked *produce* in the empty
icebox, sponged the blood speck
from its tip. The fog pushed at the windows
with a sickening heave. I picked
another moth from the drain.

To pick a moth from a sink
for the pain its flight might waken
in the mind's tepid stagnation
is a desperate act.
But last night I sat on the concrete floor
watching flies on the toilet seat,
and listened to my father, who was up
in the loft breathing hayseed
and waving his .38 at the place
where the north star should have been—
shouting at my cousin who'd gone down
to Santa Cruz with scabs
the size of nickels on her feet
to trade her baby for someone's Porsche,
and I have forgotten
what it is to be human.
What it is to be human:
I forget the dusted wings, the whiff
of sage on the fog; I forget
that an action could be made
to make meaning.

Did I choose
the humiliation of my own blood,
this hiding in shirtsleeves?

*

9

If this moth could shock me
I might remember that half-thought
before I smoked my first cigarette
at the top of the vineyard
fifteen years ago—that split
second when I sensed
I was choosing—or that fleeting
tug the first night I rummaged
in the tack room for a horse needle.

There is a strange world
in the changing of a light bulb,
the waxing of a bookshelf
I think I could grow by,
as into a dusty dream
in which each day layers
against one just past
and molds the one to come,
content as cabbage
drudging towards harvest.

It may be too far
to get to.
This morning my sister's children
knocked on the door—
I said I was sleeping; my eyes
were crusted wild and they said "but
Aunt Jane, we don't have
mud on our feet, please
can't we come in?"

*

Their terrifying, trusting voices
come back and back.

If I stepped outside
now, I could watch them
pedaling up and down
the foggy rows of vines,
their eyes clear
and open wide. Someday
I would like to write something
beautiful for them,
a song of order, undrunk,
but livable, a song
of frogs tonguing into themselves
the quiet deaths of flies, of nights
needing days, a song
equal to this season.

# Where the Zinfandel Pass Their Seasons in Mute Rows

The night Ed died, my father
wrenched his own
cracked, yellow molars
from his mouth and went
crashing like a wounded deer
over the ridge and down,
five miles through the brush,
into Soda Canyon where the cops
found him wandering, spent,
around the burnt-out dance hall
and brought him home.

Bandaging his brush cuts,
I noticed how he is becoming
the sharp-bodied boy he was
when he ran these hills
until he knew them better
than he knew his own father,
who knew them better than
the shape of *his* father's hands.

Then I watched him bend into sleep—
embryo of the king bed,
fetus with dust guts.

On the day of Ed's funeral
he gave me those teeth
"for earrings" he said, "no good
to Ed, or even to me, now."

We buried Ed with manzanita
and bay, those plants
he loved most—our own wish

for *something* to hold forever,
some way to be, in the end,
anything but alone and incomplete.

This dawn I walked
the red mud, looking
for something I could know
would never leave me—
out through the vineyard
where my father tempts life
from dirt to wine in a habit
of seasons stronger than love.
Setting my palms into the mud
at the base of a gnarled vine,
I pressed them together
and whispered "speak."
But the vine's silence just grew
into the silence of the dead
who once tended it.

Then I saw exactly how
it was beautiful—
how it held its world whole
beneath its fog-slick bark,
while the things we ask
to hold us leave us
spent. My handprints in the mud
filled with water and melted
away and my palms—done with prayer,
held out between the earth
and the sky—were empty
and red, and drying into a map.
I flexed them. The rivers widened.

# On the Lawn at the Drug Rehab Center

*To my father*

Because the wooden lawn statues
here—the bear "whose tail
could be an emerging turd" says Gale,
the squatting monkey, the cow
with taut udders—are all vaguely
obscene, this lawn is not quite
institutional. We sit, half a family
in a circle, Gale, Richie and I
—with our father, dad—groping
awkwardly back to each other.

You ask our ages: we are
older than you thought, much.
You offer us each a small cigar
and ask if we are happy.

The blue smoke turns to water
in my lungs. Gale brings out
the pornographic comics she's working on,
in which her history teacher
meets an embarrassing end.
The teacher's kidnapped—ransom set.
Nobody pays. The ransom is reduced
and reduced again. It would be awful—
ransom demanded and nobody
so much as notices. We laugh.

You say our faces,
the night we came to lock you up,
made a beautiful circle
around you. And then you stop
and I see it coming—"What

do you want from me anyway, you fucking
kidnappers?" I'll tell you. Exactly.

I want you to tell the truth—
our faces were *not* beautiful.
Truth is you fired five shots
and we scattered. Behind the stone
pillar between the vineyard
and the house I thought, that night,
of how you taught us, years ago,
to stand quietly among the vines,
to close our eyes and listen
with our feet to the sound
of the grapes growing. I listened
and I didn't hear them, father.
I heard the words
I'd read on intervention theory—
"Tell the addict how he has
let you down. Have specific
examples ready." Useless.
But we went after you again.

I know there are rooms in the mind
anyone can walk into—
I'm not saying they're any worse
than this strange lawn,
or any better,
but if you want to march
methodically into that complicated
place, I want you
to stand up first, to shake my hand
and say good-bye.

# My Father's Flesh

I know the things I know:
my father's flesh will not
keep him warm much longer.
He cannot say why
he hates it.

The worms are
working their way to his heart.
Every day there are more of them
inside him. They enter
his white arms and leave
their red tracks.

Their red tracks
scorch me when I go to hug him
and a black mouth ruptures
on my forehead. It
will not stop laughing.
I cannot find my hat.
Worms. Mouth. Scorch.

I cannot find my hat.
The mouth laughs and laughs—
uncontrollable as a dog
barking at a fire. I say
"love." The mouth snarls
"fool." I say "but love,
*love.*" My father watches.

For all I can say
I am just a woman
on fire. My father's flesh
cannot keep him warm

enough. I cannot say why
he hates it but I know
the things I know: I am
just a woman, burning.

# To the Memory

of J.S. Bach because on bad nights
I take my three brown dogs to bed
with a box of crackers, which we share
while I sing them their favorite song:

*Sheep may safely graze on pasture*
*when their shepherd guards them well.*
*Sheep may safely graze on pasture...*

I have lived by how this is funny.
I address myself to the dead now.

My body thinks she is the moon—the moon
as remembered against the metal bars
of a bridge whose arc we trust
the more the less we can.

From a distance the cars move to music.
From a distance the world sings back.

My body thinks she is the moon
but she is a clown and I
am all music and unbearably
weighted down. My small dog

on the pillow, upside down,
wiggles her feet, my mean dog
would kill for me, my old dog
cries all night for me to kill her.

Johann Sebastian Bach—
from here I can't speak back.

# Substance Abuse Trial

He mispronounces you,
the judge, rhyming your first
with your second name,
making you into something
ridiculous: Gillis Willis Mead.

But you stand as still
as they taught you in the army
when you were a young man trying hard
to keep secret what you knew
about how to kill with germs.
As quietly as we used to stand
on the front porch together at dusk
listening for the first cricket of the evening.

Now you stand accused
of wanting to die, of saying so
endlessly, with needles—and the speechless
track marks recording it all.

The evidence is
a red river, mounting.
It wants to carry you
away like an old chair
some fisherman forgot
to take home. And I want
to shout: listen
        —this man
        is my father.
        I love him.

Is there a place
where all those things

that catch in the throat
gather and shape themselves
into something as soft
as the G in Giles
was meant to be pronounced?

Is *that* where you thought
you were going?

# To Nobody: February 20, 1985

*(On the way to K Mart to buy a filing cabinet.)*

What I wanted was a solid exchange
of cash for steel, but
the surcharge—that hallucinatory
exchange of pleasantries
that turns existence to the air
around a curtsy—was more
than I could pay
and I kept driving.
The white fields
have a world to themselves,
but human silence needs
a human shelf, so I depended
on the way I knew—
each time I shifted gears—
the team of Swedes
who made my car and, trusting
only that solid connection,
drove. Here at the Stagsfoot
Motel, I'll M.C.
my life tonight. No more
smiles at the register, no more
false currency. Disregard
is a counterfeit word:
the things we choose
to do define us. So,
while I may choose,
one day, to forgive her,
I do not mourn Sarah.
    August 1, 1977.
    Heroin.
    Or Reed.
    June 18, 1978.
    O.D.'d.

I do not mourn Paul.
November 15, 1983.
D.O.A.
Or Dad.
Missing.
Twenty-nine days now.

You cowards.

I have snapped the back
of this year in some town
I do not care to know
the name of. Here
at the Stagsfoot
hoof
paw
jaw
breath of mildew
where I'm M.C.,
keeper of the key
to room one-o-one,
I do not even mourn
the voices between my ears
or care
why they cut out.
You cowards.

What I wanted was steel and square.
Cash for gas.
Grease for gears.

# After Detox

*"For ten days panic will claw your face, then it will be over."*

I like the pale light best: the light of dusk
and the light of dawn. And in the hours between—the soft
yellow in the light of closed eyes. On my back,
sometimes I clench them for flashes—like worrying
the red dictionary for words—that don't cut
deep enough. My arms have finally released
my body. My body has fallen back into itself,
fallen into an undisturbed place where nerves
lead nowhere. I think—life. I think—death.
Laundry, I think. Eat. Laundry. Death. Eat.
The light comes softly around curtains; the light
leaves slowly, leaking out around curtains. The sun
is rising and falling. No dying claims my thoughts;
no gem of whisky, no flower of opium
names them. I do my laundry every evening,
walk mechanically down the faded street to where the warm
machines rattle and hum, and the warm soap splashes
behind glass. A life as clean as a bed.
A bed in a room. My hand goes out to touch
a teacup. It is there. Nothing moves in the pure
dim behind my eyes, where thoughts once darted. I wait.
My socks will match. My hair will shine. I like
the pale light best. The light of dusk and the light of dawn.
It seeps around my life slowly. It leaves
without knocking. It has no ending and no beginning,
and all the rest—that other death they call living.

II

*"Living"*

Everybody in my family has something he must do
to hold us all up; two days after my mother
took me home I had my old job back. I work
at a diner. Luci's Place—with a lot of road traffic
and some regulars. Luci's Place—with sunflowers
between the parking lot and the light green
concrete-block wall; in summer their stems bend
under the huge weight of blossoms. I hide
under grubby clatter; I work at a diner
on the outskirts of town, but it's the green glare
of trees—which hurts my eyes—I died for.

In the morning, sitting in my nightgown by the window,
I watch the light seep around the corners of Glen's Garage.
Yellow, orange, blue. Colors of the rainbow
or the sky rising. Colors on the rusted plates
on the rusted cars. Cars with their toes turned up,
tires sold, fenders missing. Cars from all over, with maps
of stars on the windshields where heads have smashed.

I read stories full of people with descriptions—
some of them have noses that are big, eyes that are small,
skin that is bad, but noses, eyes and skin somebody
has bothered to describe. I try to think of my life in plot.
Bamboozled. But I laugh, for I know that the sunflowers
and the old cars with the pale light at their edges
are all the beauty I'll ever need to hold me up.

*

I speak softly to the light when its white hands
warm my cheeks. I speak softly to the world,
but I can never explain the way life fades
as it approaches, the way, mid-sentence, I'll realize
it's not me who is speaking, and listen
to the strange words of a strange voice. Or the way
what it is that I'm meant to be doing is always
just on the tip of my tongue. Or why I began
in the northwest quadrant of my forehead,
just above the hairline, and carved, with mother's
dullest knife, the long diagonal line that ends
at the right side of my jaw. Or how the wide red scar
—its shiny translucent skin—turned out
exactly as I wanted. I can never explain,
but it should speak for itself—the map
of a vision, proof that I exist. It's only honest—
to wear your skin as if it were your own.

# The Memory

The body refuses to die.
The soul refuses to be stronger.
The memory I cannot fully form
will never fully leave me—
the memory of a man who tried to save me:
vague curve of shoulders and back
disappearing down the playground path
between snowdrifts. Swingchains
on my hands in winter.

*Come back—there must be something*
*you must have forgotten—.*

Did he wear a red scarf?
Was he shoeless in the snow?
He had a three day's beard—or, no—
he was clean-shaven. He bent over.
With his warm breath he unfroze
my hands from the swingchains—
not pulling till they were ready.

If only he would tell me now:
What does it mean to let go?

Sometimes a strange feeling comes over me.
My body tingles as if it were alone
with the soul, trying to explain to her
its inability. She understands.
She needs something.

Why is she not complete?
What does she need to be complete?
Ask the present, ask the body. No,

ask the blurred snowdrift darkening, quick—
ask the child on the swingset; she knows.

It was a red scarf.
Yes, and the wind blew it as he bent over
and the knees of his unbelted pants were baggy.
His breath loosened my hands from the chains,
from the swingset. He whispered
"let go."

Then he turned and walked sadly
down the playground path and suddenly,
in the tired curve of a back,
my body recognized itself.

Nothing more. Nothing forgotten.

It seems wrong—
the way the body refuses to die.
It seems wrong—
the way the soul refuses to be stronger.

There should have been something more.
A binding word perhaps—*body, sorrow*—
or a parting glance dissolving—
*too late, too late, too late.*

But now, at least, there is nothing
between me and my soul but myself.

# To the Body

I don't know how to speak to you.
I have tried and tried, but I don't
know how to answer.

I gave you tide pools for your feet,
salt on wind for your lips
and the sound of waves for your ears:

Nothing.

I made you stare through the arch of a window
where Simon left his body hanging:
Nothing, not a tremor.

I tried the junkie's twilight sleep,
but you would not come with me. I climbed
the stairs in a house by the sea.

Climbed past the porthole on the landing,
the tailless lizard in the corner,
and let the stranger's hands massage you.

I forgot myself and let her have you.
These things I did for you because of what I know:
there is no easy truce of words forthcoming.

And you just pushed the clear tears out—
they dripped down the bench to the carpet—
they kept on coming—as if I'd understand.

As if I'd understand or could go with you.

# ▪ TWO ▪

# Sparrow, My Sparrow

The voice that loves me best when I am dreaming
comes from every corner of the circle of my sleep
speaking in the sound of my own drowning.
She says *the body's just a habit getting old,*
*a crystal turning on a nerve of ancient longing.*
She says *I will teach you how to be with yourself*
*always,* she says *we do not live in the same world.*

All this is just an allegory for the truth.
Truth is, I cannot speak
the voice that I've been dreaming.
Truth is, the slate sky darkens,
clouds of sparrows heave in the wind,
the trees are massed with sparrows screaming
and the fields are dotted with them.
The birds are bracing themselves. The birds
are frenzied by something about to happen.

Truth is, I have my feet on the slimy banks.
I look for my face in the murk-green river
and the water's surface does not change.

But I hear myself in the screech of sparrows
and am panicked by something about to happen.

Slate sky—darkened; sound in wind:
I enter this world like myself as a prayer.
I enter this world as myself.
I cannot help myself.

What is a prayer but a song of longing
turning on the thread of its own history?
*

I feel myself loved by a voice in the wind—
I cover my ears with my palms.
The whole world rocks and still
the cold green river does not spill.

# Mapping the Mind

One thing I know for certain—
there's a slow green river
I've been living by.

Not the banks: in their green-gold light
there's a message I can't read.

Not the carp those fishermen
keep leaving on the shore—
though because I know raccoons
have been eating carp eyes in the night
my life must be imperceptibly changed.

No. Not the banks, not the carp—
and not the vine-tangled trees.
I do not love them—though I love
how the river reflects them.

This green line, then, will stand
for the river and the river
running through me.

Now, what will the banks be?
I must marry them to me.
A river needs banks or it has no course.

What will the banks be,
and how will I know when I have found them?

And when I have drawn them in, then,
where will my soul be—
who must surely be returning
else she would have taken me with her.

\*

Wouldn't she?

She must surely be returning.

I can draw a solitary bird
circling her reflection in the river.

Now let her enter.

# In Need of a World

Who wouldn't want a life
made real by the passage of time
or a world, at least,
made real by the mind. Something
solid and outer, though connected.

Who wouldn't want to know
for certain how to get there?

I'd like to tell you simply
how I passed this day putting tomatoes up,
or how I tied a stern cicada to a string
so I could feel the gentle tug
its flying in frantic circles made.

I'd like to show you the red
worm-shaped burn on my wrist
and in this way claim myself.

Instead I slip out of my every day—
away into the distant and lulling sound
of "once-upon-a-time-there-was-a-woman."

Will I ever find that perfect stance
of soul and mind from which sparks
a self uttering itself?
I'm always slipping between rows of corn—
through the field that rises toward this ridge
from which I like the houses for their smallness.

Here I lean against a Honey Locust,
feathery tree with its three-inch thorns,
and watch sagging strands of barbed wire

sway slightly in the wind—the clump
of brown fur hanging there, waving.

I watch the field of drying corn beyond,
and beyond that the soccer field
and rows of clean-lined condos.
I wait for the yellow light to flick on
in the white church across the valley.

Will I ever learn the way to love
the ordinary things I love to look at?

I'm always slipping away
between rows of corn, climbing
toward this ridge to think,
when really what I want is a ridge
or a lonely field on the edge of the world
of the mind. A place from which to speak
honestly to that man on the porch, a way
to greet the children who are swinging
on the edge of dusk behind chain-link fences.

But always it's either I or world.
World or I.

And when it's I, I'm dreaming
on a quiet ridge that the tomatoes
ripened and, though I was missing,
a woman put an apron on and canned them.

And when it's world, it pushes me back
towards that madness of the soul
which is not a field, nor a ridge, nor a way.

# Begin Where We All Know Which and Where We Are

I

*Carquinez, Dumbarton, Benicia and Bay*

It begins with the world and its many bridges
receding, and how you make a song to hold it,
how you sing out loud for all you're worth—
*Carquinez, Dumbarton, Benicia and Bay*—and how
then even the song goes off beyond static.

And you know that it's the body's story rising
up to meet you, here where you're wrong in life,
so you sweep dead bugs from the window ledge
with the knife edge of your hand just to see the arc
your arm makes, and feel the powdered wings if you can.

But still there's just a literal numbness spreading
so you try to think where you lost your foothold,
but you can't cover the distance back, or out
to where the red wing flickers in the air
on the dull mat of sky, that faded square.

And you know that elsewhere there's another body
fallen, and it's the body of your own dismay
in a bright and drizzly season under thunder,
against the dark face of a cliff, and you think
perhaps the way back in would be to go there.

And when you get there the place has changed some:
you note the branches and the good sun shining,
how the yellow star thistles make a field; you note
the many Ceanothus in the Ceanothus bush,
you the looker looking—and never arriving.

*

So you stay with that thought for as long as you can,
yo-yoing out to the brim and back in, back
to where you began, where you fed your dogs
which was a prayer for the world to begin, for the body
to mention herself: *here, here, I'm over here.*

But she isn't stirring so you try the memory:
the middle of Iowa, the middle of winter, the middle
of the night, snow on the baseball field, moonlight on it,
how it came to you: so *this* is the world. You
remember too how it was gone by morning.

The quail are scruffing in the underbrush,
you think that's got to do with why you're here—
but it isn't any good and it's taken everything
you have to trust it, and meanwhile you're
just waiting and it gets to be a long time.


II

*The Body's Story Rising*


If you want to tell the story of what happens
when sound waves don't share a common center
you could begin with how, in 1842,
Christian Johan Doppler loaded a flatcar
with fifteen professional trumpeters
and rolled them by a stationary listener.

You could begin with the image of a trumpet
in sunlight, the sound of a symphony

over the sound of wheel on rail, steel
on steel. However you begin, however much
you want to keep them reading, it will all return,
in the end, to where you started, what you know.

The sound, say, of an ambulance missing the driveway.
Try mentioning the cottonwood swaying in the night—
leaving out the window too small to crawl through—
and pretty soon you'll see what the cottonwood's for,
it's there because you need to tell what happened,
you need to keep them long enough to hurt them.

Sooner or later, you'll get to the ambulance—
and the man in the house who keeps beating the woman.
The worst part then will be your refusal
to stop telling it. The worst part will be
their refusal to read on. The worst part
is the way you need to hurt them.

You thought the words arriving is what kept you,
but suddenly you're crazy with the image
on the edge, how it's got to be maintained, how
it's the last place there is for those who live there—
and you start with caution, you start
with naked women running on the beach.

You describe the waves and the pretty sky,
you say the sun is setting, justify the lie,
because you know you're going to bring the men in,
you know it's about soldiers slashing the women
from behind as they are running, you know
and so you promise sex from the beginning.

*

And before you know it, before they know it,
you've moved from the dream to the truth
about how some of the women enter the water
bleeding, about what happened to the ones
who never get there. Who are you losing?
Some of us enter the water bleeding.

We swim and they follow. We wake in prison
because we do not know whose side we're on.
We're the one who leads the keeper to the cell.
The one who lets him in, and the woman
with the dead face lying there, her too.
We know the significance of her henna hair.

We know it will happen before he rapes her,
how the slick of semen on her crotch
matches exactly the glaze on her eyes, body
like a board—you know the feeling? Body
as the lie you live by, a pronoun
as a hundred pounds of meat in search of meaning.

You end with the image of the bruise he made,
how she jabs it just to keep it, how it's
how she holds her place, how you hold your place.
This is the story of twenty-one years spent
looking for a place to put my hands, a way
to be here, practicing the posture of erasure.

There are whole days I spend with music.
Afternoons made of my need to go there.
Just that now, and the image of a bruise,

its many paths receding—the body as bruise,
the bruise as the story, and the story
as the answer to not being here.

# A Note on the Present State of the Future

Just when he's finally buttering her a roll
it will occur to me, these aren't
rock trucks I've been hearing, not

their routine squall as they near the hairpin
and see the cliff approaching.  Same rumble
but trucks going up. I'll close the book

and realize it's fire trucks—
sirens off for the long heave
through the country. And when the lights go out

I'll know: you *could* gather rocks
in this kind of moonlight, you could
do it just to do it and be glad.

When I call the man at P G & E he'll say
my power's out, they're getting to it, and
now that you ask, yes, there *is* a fire

and when I call the man at Forestry
he'll be a recording concerning the need
for permits and inspection of burning sites,

ending with a number for Forestry 2,
who will tell me my power's out. I
won't ask him to come and spend the night,

won't even tell him how I know—
when this hill goes up in flames
it goes, nothing left of this house

*

eight years ago but some concrete steps.
Instead, I'll just say thanks, and try
to dump this all in one final guffaw

and run—like thinking about electricity
and fire and how when transformers blow it looks
and sounds like the Fourth of July. Meanwhile, I'm

working by candlelight on a description
of fire, taking comfort in the notion
of the poverty of description, doodling

in the margins—stairs going down, which is
as far as my not-so-famous talent takes me:
There's a pit at the end of every thought

and it wants me like Br'er Rabbit's
*anything*. Anything. For example,
the thought of what I cannot do—the one

about two women, one who is *other*
and the other, who is beaten,—and the pit
saying choose. Or a thought for a poem that ends

with the speaker wondering briefly
why she's still alone, then reopening the novel
at the spot where a man hands a woman a roll,

and how she will read by the light of the moon,
and how then she will read by the approaching fire,—
the whole thing insisting on closure now,

*

when somewhere there's still an image
on the loose—the one that contains the moment
at which she might say *might*—say *yes*, say *no*.

# To Vincent Van Gogh
# of the House He Painted
# in 1890, the Year of His Death

This evening my valley has the colors
of your "House at Auvers"—your colors,
my colors now. Fog smudges up from the bay
and is lost in the blue-green fields—
it's the color of the lake through mist, color
of the smoke from five damp trash fires
which drifts up towards elsewhere, taking
its time. This is the color you gave
your sky, this is the color you gave
your house. The greens I see are the ones *you* chose
for roof and shrubs and shutters, and I—
in my red flannel shirt—could be
the flame of poppies you put in the corner.

Except that nothing human strays there—
there is no sign of human life at all.

I have come from planting blackberries,
sunflowers and cabbages—planting them
to hold me here a while longer,
in this house overlooking the valley.

The valley is fading in dusk and warm rain.

All the houses are dropping away. They are leaving
too fast. What if we never have our moment?

And what if it's all there—in your painting—
what if there *is* no missing gesture? What

if a shovel left by the gate would not have done,
if putting it there could not have saved you?

And if it's *not* the absence in your windows
of a frail hand pulling curtains back,
of a face, half-shadowed, looking toward you—
then it must be that you knew too well
just how to make the sagging woodshed lovely.

The world is still much larger than itself.
The world is still unbearable or small:
greens, blues, flame of poppies, smoke
rising up toward elsewhere—taking its time.

# Bach, Winter

Bach must have known—how
something flutters away when you turn
to face the face you caught sideways
in a mirror, in a hall, at dusk—

and how the smell of apples in a bowl
can stop the heart for an instant,
between sink and stove,
in the dead of winter when stars

of ice have spread across the windows
and everything is perfectly still
until you catch the sound of something
lost and shy beating its wings.

And then: music.

# Paradise Consists of Forty-Nine Rotating Spheres

paradise gave me these legs
    for spinning
weep and pray and be joyful
paradise gave me these legs
    to weep and pray and be joyful

when I have fixed each corner
    p l i é  relevé spin
I start the silky spokes
      p l i é  relevé spin

paradise gave me these legs
    to weep and pray
               I am joyful

    youthful youthful
        paradise gave me these legs
so I spin
    black nights
      blue days
              p l i é  relevé spin
my web against the sky

    a perfect circle shakes the stars
mine's a pure imitation
    sung from planets of memory
      spun from threads of dreams
weep and pray and be joyful

    paradise gave me these legs
that's all I need to know
paradise gave me these legs
    for spinning

I have spun
forty-nine webs of silken threads
my window to the sky

# LaGuardia, the Story

I

A man in the clot of colors—which are people—
is holding a naked iris, is watching
the long line of faces unloading.

He holds the flower up to his chest, then
down at a tilt to his side—in one hand
behind his back makes a surprise.

He runs through his posture
now and again. He uses
one shoe at a time for standing.

The long line of faces—its trickle and blurt—
hurts me. He is watching for her face.

She must have sat at the back of the plane—
a seven-forty-seven: she's been smoking.
Perhaps something has happened that matters.
Perhaps what has happened is nothing—
but the face that arrives is never
the face that left us. Remember that.

I want to rest my head on his back,
on his blue flannel shirt. I imagine
her face which must arrive. I imagine
that she must not disappoint him.

Will I know her before he sees her?
What does their story mean to me?

*

I used to walk through Kensington Gardens
every morning on my way to school
that winter we lived at Lancaster Gate.
*This* is a story too—does it have meaning,
is it about something that matters—does it
tell how the branches aged the white sky?

Is its secret in the fog or the red sun rising,
in the ducks on the Serpentine as seen
through a layer of mist—can it explain
why my mother whimpered in her sleep that year?

In the frame story she walks off last,
sees the flower—hands up for a moment
for *surprise* before she takes it.

She gives him a small kiss and they head off
arm in arm down the long hall
happily, until I can no longer see them.

This is the story as I saw it happen.
The story as I told it.

In their second story he waits with the iris
long after she doesn't arrive—
but for some other reason than for
so-I-can-save-him: she has been delayed—
perhaps by something inconsequential,
we don't know yet, but in the second story

she does not arrive. This is the story
as I imagine it—the story that exists.

Is there any other possible story?

Walking home from school in the afternoons
I'd stop and sit by the Serpentine
and rub my fingers on the curbstone.
I loved the raw circles I made in their tips—
symmetrical and red as the skin
under the popped bubble of a blister.

Is there any other story possible?
Who must I be to make her exist?

## II

I am stuck in the middle of the story,
not knowing if she will arrive.
I saw her face, this makes no difference—
there is a man at LaGuardia
holding an iris. When I think of it
I cannot stop fearing for him.

How do you unlock a story? How
do you recognize the image—
the one that might change you?

If I put in the part about my mother
and step-father fighting, if I describe
—perfectly—his body in action,
his shadow on the wall behind him,
or add the bit about it all boiling down
to inquisitions in the rational morning—as in
whose dark anus holds the safe-box key—
will we have a story with a meaning?

There is a way to discover a truth
about anything you want to know.

I imagine there's a way to know what's real.

Listen—I walked through an empty park
every morning on my way to school
and knew that it was good to be human.

*

Some nights I make a killer pot of coffee—
I put on the music that I love,
and dance. Sometimes I dance for hours.

Go to your phonograph. Put on
Brandenburg Concerto Number Six.

This is about something very hard.
—This is about trying to live with that music
playing in the back of your mind.

—About trying to live in a world
with that kind of music.

# ▪ THREE ▪

# Between Self and Century

This is the century of the one lost shoe
at the side of the highway, century
of the old shoe curled back at the toe,
sole split, the usual mud-streaked heel.

This is the century of the big black oak
at the far end of this field of gold,
oak blurred by the air between us—
looking like a cloud of smoke, black
against the white smoke that is the sky.


\* \* \*


I wanted to be the girl doing leg-lifts
in front of the evening news, the one
who's up on current events, but countries
I don't recognize the names of keep falling
and I'm between field and highway with the names
of those countries burning into my skull.

I'm the one who's always fasting
as if God would then come in,
the one with twigs snarled in her hair
watching a penful of pigs.
They lie in the mud shitting themselves
and squinting at me. I love them
because nothing can do *pig* as well as pig
and I am lost and do not know who I am, or if
life has anything to do with prayer.

\* \* \*

The man who called me yellow-bird
had nothing to do with me.
He called me that because *he* wanted to fly
just as my sister called me limbs
so she would not have to love me.

But they had nothing to do with me.

There ought to be an image around here somewhere
with its back pushed up snug against that cloud,
an image to hold the world up, refusing
to shrug, refusing, even, to weep.

But this is the century of the old shoe.

\* \* \*

There must have been something I loved once.
Some thing I made bright.

I think of the yellow curtains I made
for the kitchen of a small brown house.
A house that sat on the edge of a river.
Every morning my hands swept them open.
Every evening I closed them again.

Yes, it was the yellow checked curtains I made
so carefully—crooked to match the crooked house.
\*

I must still be the woman who pulled curtains back.
I must be the road back into myself.

There must be something there. I loved
the motion of hands letting light in,
my own hands sweeping curtains back,
arching across the arc of the morning,
two white doves at the window, looking out
and the tide of light pouring in.

# The Argument against Us

The line of a man's neck, bent
over welding, torchlight breaking
shadows on his face, hands cracked
into a parched map of fields he has woken—
the gods wanted us.

Think of their patient preparation:
the creature who left the rocking waves behind,
crawling up on some beach, the sun
suddenly becoming clear. Small thing
abandoning water for air, crooked body
not quite fit for either world, but the one
that finally made it. Think of all the others.

Much later, spine uncurls, jaw pulls back, brow-bone
recedes, and as day breaks over the dry plain
a rebellious boy takes an upright step
where primitive birds are shrieking above him.

He did it for nothing. He did it
against all odds. Bone of wrist, twist
of tooth, angel of atoms—an infinity
of courage sorted into fact
against the shining backdrop of the world.

The line of one man's neck, bent—
torchlight breaking shadows on his face.

There was a creature who left the waves behind
and a naked child on a windy plain:
when the atom rips out into our only world

and we're carried away on a wave of hot wind
I will love them no less: they are just how much
the gods wanted us.

# For Alex at the Gladman Memorial Hospital

Because he is kicking and knows
he's not going to make it, Alex
is in love with what he's painting.

He's got the mountain in, and the
mountain-and-sky-in-the-lake, is saving
all of tomorrow for the upper sky, because

"With that you got to take your time."
There's something broken, something
whole in how he says it, and something

he's working on mending, like
how the black line of shore runs
between mountains, like

knowing that whatever we're wanting
is not far from here—no farther, maybe,
than the fix he'll get to fix it when they

throw up their hands at his mum pastorals
and boot him out. He doesn't know
shit from you-know-what about shoes

but he's familiar with the facts upstream,
knows the paint on the Golden Gate
is poisonous and that here he wants

to use blues that refer to each other—
as in lake-blue mountain and what's
going to be the mountain-blue sky when
*

and if he gets there. He wants
to agree with his body. He
wants to know if it's a bad gene,

or if it's got to do with signs
and the times—with the century
writ small enough to piss on.

But even if we *are* the scene
behind this scene, I'm still not going
to leave you with that squint from a distance

through some gritty air where bridge
and sandblaster meet as something like
*a pale cloud of golden mist and the bay*

*below calm as a lily, but gray—*
or with *gold close the mountain*
*and part ways with syntax* though

they're a fix of sorts. No, if you
follow this road as far as you can,
you will arrive at a blotch, which,

if it's in the foreground, recommends
itself in the shade and the shape
of a bird, and, if it's in the background,

desires to desire to depict miles
of bay-blue sky, by Alex. Alex—
wrapped in a blanket, a man describing

\*

a painting, clumsily describing
his many careful brushstrokes, his
long reach out toward something true—

without turning elsewhere, which is
indebtedness, which is annihilation
when we can call it anything we want.

# The Man in the Poetry Lounge

at Berkeley is reading English
pastoral poetry with passive
abandon, chewing his thumbnail
aggressively. He wants

to see grass, he wants to
BE grass so badly he can
almost smell it. Outside,
they are cutting the grass—

the man and the mower—they are
dressing and keeping the garden.
They are not far enough away
from my hayfever, but the man

reading pastorals is off—
zeroing in on calmer places.
Have the birds arrived yet?
Have the larks and nightingales

made their appearance? I would like
to ask him to let me know
when he gets to the birds. I would like
to concentrate then and there, and lose

what I have read about Flanders
and Picardy and the trenches of WW I:
the larks appearing around the time
of stand-to in the morning,

the nightingales showing up
by stand-to at night. I would like never

to have learned that they were there.
But instead, because my nose is running,

my eyes are getting smaller by the minute,
and I'm edgy, I'll ask him sweetly
if he's bothered at home
by bedbugs, rats, or lice,

and justify the question with an explanation:
I myself am bothered by fleas.
This is why I keep scratching—
which act I hope he does not find

distracting because, really,
who am I to ruin his birds.
I who cannot, as you have seen,
follow those trenches to their

logical conclusion. Instead, I too
have searched long, and found
that in the gentle arc
of a pig's back there really is

a thought to calm the thinker—
if, that is, the pig be tame.
I want to know if this man
loves what he is reading—

and if he loves it enough
in what way it will change him.
Are we onto something real now
or is this all about planting

\*

a false goose in front of the moon?
Do the iambs soothe him? Is he
big on true rhyme and false conclusion,
the sonic hanky—you wipe your eyes

you blow your nose. Which I will
have to leave this room to do.
But not before I've resisted
coming right out and asking

if he's fulfilling the requirements
of heart or mind, and asked instead
what it's my true right to know
(involving, as it does, the heat

of concentration, the problem
of public safety, as in MY safety):
if his shirt, which I'll begin
by calling handsome, has passed

the requirements of the Flammable
Fabrics Act. Then I'll
step out and blow my nose,
at which point I might as well wander

back on down toward Cody's and try
to receive the world, browsing
and scratching in the poetry section,
after buying a paper poppy for a dollar—

the one you didn't want to know was coming—
the Flanders—from a veteran of foreign wars

at Telegraph and Durant—not,
of course, looking at his left leg—

because I can't.
Because it isn't there.

# The Case of the Misplaced Caption

You can take it back now, not
as in beginning *in medias res*,
but as in your desire for a plot—

because if what you want to know
is that on January 17 of some
new year Toyotas went on sale

in Sacramento, where there was
a subplot involving the San
Francisco dealer, and I

saw the dentist, nine a.m.,
perfect teeth, and war, what?
broke out? having repercussions

throughout the economy, the immediate
universe, our teeth, our Toyotas, our
ability to keep both body and soul,

then I offer you this:
she looks into the camera
out at all America and says

*I'm sure he'll come back, he's
a good soldier.* Listen.
Listen to it. The

marriage is over folks.
Read it in *Redbook*, read it
in *McCall's*, read it at the dentist:

\*

*A noted royal biographer*
*creates a correspondence*
*that takes us inside*

*the hearts and minds of*
*Charles and Diana.*
Or, seen the other way—

*New York Times* best seller
number eleven, *The Secret*
*Diary of Laura Palmer:*

put it on your night-stand
put it in your hand, your head,
put yourself in the story—

eight ninety-five, which is
not nine, but rather the marriage
of psychology and economics

at some small expense to small us.
And then there's what we're down to—
*ABC pulls episode of spy show:*

"It's so close to what's going on
we didn't want to run it, it
could scare the hell out of people."

Lady, you might not want him back,
and it's not your fault, but
this isn't the chapter

*

where the witch gets roasted— no trail
of crumbs in this forest, just you
and how you *really*

might not want him back, not
alive, that is, and that
when I tell you just how he

held the gun, aimed the camera,
made the lens, wrote the story,
sold the magazine, or mention

that he went down with his
arms around his child,
we've reached the six-he level

of pronoun saturation, meaning
you can either be a good
soldier and put this down

or continue on into *who
couldn't he be?* You see
there's an agenda

under the agenda, having
to do with how both *taken*
and *image* reside

in the case of the hero's
photo, having to do
with the universal rights of man,—

\*

and it moves to a logic that goes
like this: *In the event*
*of multiple losses resulting*

*from the same accident*
*only one amount is payable—*
*the largest amount applicable,*

which is what the dead
say to the living in the moment
before the gun goes off:

you have the right to silence,
you have the right to the ashes
on your hands, the ashes

that are your hands. Christ,
your rights, your vote, your
recycle bins, your desire

for a plot. You
can take them back. This
is my body, I offer it

to the dead now. Let the
stars go on with their stories.

It was love that led me here.

# In the Parking Lot at the Junior College on the Eve of a Presidential Election

I've been sitting in this parking lot
for a long time—thinking
about nothing. The bumper sticker
on the car next to mine reads
BORN TO SHOP, and makes me wonder
why I can't laugh too—why I
can't laugh with the best of us.

There's a small New Testament,
bound in calf, on my dashboard—
someone I love has died and left me
with it, a cryptic trail guide
to some foreign land.

Once upon a time there was
a man named Abraham. (At first
he seemed like an ordinary man.)

*He begat Isaac who begat*
*Jacob who begat Judah and his brethren.*
*Then Perez and Zerah of Tamar.*

And the song on a radio blaring past—
 Talking about the splendour
 of the Hoover Factory—
 know that you'd agree
 if you had seen it too.

*Hezron, Ram, Amminadab.*
*Nahshon, Salmon, Boaz of Rahab,*
*Obed, Jesse and David the King...*

*

Five miles out of London
on the Western Avenue—
must have been a wonder
when it was brand new.

*Manasseh, Amon, Josiah, Jechoniah*—
Jechoniah of the time
of the carrying away to Babylon.

And what might there be for us
now that Babylon has been blown
all the way to Coventry?

What might there be now for us?
Some small prayer—some bold
giving over of what remains?

*And Jechoniah begat Shealtiel
who begat Zerubbabel.*

I, like you, am tired
of names. There are so many
names, and we are so impatient.
We are so important!

Yesterday my fat student Marty
announced that his favorite pastime
was hanging out at McDonald's.
The whole class laughed
as if they have always known
the world was about to end.

*

They are young enough
to have known this
for the whole of their lives.

*And Joseph the husband of Mary*
*of whom was born Jesus,*
*who is called Christ.*

But who must have been,
after all, just a man.
Right?

Abraham. We could, perhaps,
have an Abraham among us.
And if it were possible
to wait for forty-two lifetimes
we might have been able
to come to something better.

Abraham. Abraham—
I'm talking about the wonder.

# Delphi, Coming around the Corner

Delphi, coming around the corner of the house,
one shoe on foot, one shoe in hand, says
he thought the dog shit was just a shadow.

This has happened before.
He scrapes it off on my door stoop, off
to the side, we wait for rain.

Meanwhile, my idea of an afternoon
is a couple of dogs chewing cow toes
in my bed—and me, and Delphi,

whom I love. Delphi, who
cannot read or write. Sometimes
I try to teach him—goes like this:

*This is my Oil of Olay, T.M., this*
*is my shell-pink polish, also T.M.ed,*
*and these are the little shrimps that are my toes.*

Later I try again. *This is the other*
*side of the story,* I say,
picking up the book and quoting:

"Writing is that (dot dot dot) space
where all identity is lost, starting with the
(dot dot dot) identity of the body writing."

*Unquote,* I say, adding a footnote[1]
just in case. Delphi puts the book
on the floor. Later I try again.

\*

---

1. Roland Barthes, *Image—Music—Text*, trans. Stephen Heath
(New York: Hill and Wang, 1977), p. 142.

*This is my poem for you,* I say,
*this is the place where I can't,*
*for a song, put the song in.* So I sing it.

Delphi sings harmony, the dogs stop chewing.
Delphi knows the end to every story,
his literal, illiterate eyelids fluttering shut.

# Passing a Truck Full of Chickens at Night on Highway Eighty

What struck me first was their panic.

Some were pulled by the wind from moving
to the ends of the stacked cages,
some had their heads blown through the bars—

and could not get them in again.
Some hung there like that—dead—
their own feathers blowing, clotting

in their faces. Then
I saw the one that made me slow some—
I lingered there beside her for five miles.

She had pushed her head through the space
between bars—to get a better view.
She had the look of a dog in the back

of a pickup, that eager look of a dog
who knows she's being taken along.
She craned her neck.

She looked around, watched me, then
strained to see over the car—strained
to see what happened beyond.

*That* is the chicken I want to be.

# ◼ Acknowledgments

Grateful acknowledgment is made to the editors and publishers of the following periodicals and anthologies in which the poems in this collection were first published, sometimes in different versions:

*American Poetry Review:* "Delphi, Coming around the Corner," "LaGuardia, the Story," and "Passing a Truck Full of Chickens at Night on Highway Eighty"
*The Antioch Review:* "In Need of a World"
*Arete: Forum for Thought:* "On the Lawn at the Drug Rehab Center" and "To Nobody: February 20, 1985"
*The Beloit Poetry Journal:* "In the Parking Lot at the Junior College on the Eve of a Presidential Election"
*The Boston Review:* "Fall" and "Sparrow, My Sparrow"
*The Iowa Review:* "For Alex at the Gladman Memorial Hospital" and "To the Body"
*The North Dakota Quarterly:* "To Vincent Van Gogh of the House He Painted in 1890, the Year of His Death"
*Pequod:* "A Note on the Present State of the Future," "Begin Where We All Know Which and Where We Are," and "After Detox" (formerly "Maybe She Go")
*Ploughshares:* "The Case of the Misplaced Caption," "Bach, Winter," "Paradise Consists of Forty-Nine Rotating Spheres," and "Where the Zinfandel Pass Their Seasons in Mute Rows"
*The Seattle Review:* "Mapping the Mind"
*The Virginia Quarterly Review:* "Concerning That Prayer I Cannot Make," "My Father's Flesh," "The Lord and the General Din of the World," "The Man in the Poetry Lounge," and "The Memory"

"Bach, Winter" was reprinted in *1986–87: Anthology of Magazine Verse and Yearbook of American Poetry*.
"Concerning That Prayer I Cannot Make" was reprinted in *The Best American Poetry of 1990*.
"Sparrow, My Sparrow" was reprinted in *Pacific International*.
"Between Self and Century," "In Need of a World" and "The Argument against Us" appeared in *Voices on the Landscape: Contemporary Iowa Poets*.

Thanks also to the Mrs. Giles Whiting Foundation, not only for the award which afforded me some time to work on these poems, but also for the timely encouragement represented by that award.

In addition, I am deeply grateful to those who have helped shape these poems and this book, and whose friendship and support have sustained me: Julie Checkoway, Ira Sadoff, Philip Booth, Tess Gallagher, Timothy Liu, Jorie Graham, Gerald Freund, Alan Williamson, Gerald Stern, Kathleen Peirce and Randall Potts.

Finally, I wish to express my gratitude to Sarah Gorham for her guidance, and most especially to Philip Levine, for taking notice of these poems in the first place.

# ◪ The Author

**Jane Mead** was educated at Vassar College, Syracuse University, and the University of Iowa Writers' Workshop and has taught at several schools in the San Francisco Bay area, at Colby College, and in the Iowa Summer Writing Festival. In 1991, State Street Press published her long poem, "A Truck Marked Flammable" as a chapbook. Her individual poems have been widely published in such places as *The New York Times, Best American Poetry of 1990, American Poetry Review, The Virginia Quarterly, Ploughshares*, and *The Antioch Review*. In 1992, she received a Whiting Writers' Award.